BITS
AND PIECES
OR HOW MY HEART SINGS

ADRIENNE CRAWFORD

authorHOUSE®

AuthorHouse™
1663 Liberty Drive
Bloomington, IN 47403
www.authorhouse.com
Phone: 1 (800) 839-8640

Published by AuthorHouse 04/23/2016

ISBN: 978-1-5246-0483-7 (sc)
ISBN: 978-1-5246-0482-0 (e)

Library of Congress Control Number: 2016906714

Print information available on the last page.

This book is printed on acid-free paper.

Dedication

And so I dedicate this book to my two moms. My mom called Mommy
Neal and my maternal aunt, Mommy Florence. Together they raised
8 children with the intermittent help from the men in their lives.
But it was mostly them. Mommy Neal the strong one, taking care of
every one and Mommy Florence, the teacher who loved everyone.

Between them they raised us to love God, value education and
believe we could reach higher than the level of our poverty.

Mommy Florence

My mom's sister the more quiet one. Left paralyzed from the
waist down by polio. Sitting in a wheelchair never to walk
again. Yet I never saw her cry or feel sorry for herself.

She was the wind beneath my mother's wings.

And between the two of them they left a legacy
for us to be great, their children.

Nealy

Mommy Neal, my mom, on us kids like white on rice. 24/7, Like
Vegas always open, She never ceased to correct us for our good. Never
tired!! Where did she get that energy? All my sisters and brothers are
fine. Achievers and helpers of others. What a inheritance she left.
Yet, she is still with us. Smiling down at me My mom.
Mommy Neal A force to be reckoned with.

Acknowledgments

First of all to my late husband, William Crawford, love of my life, gone but never forgotten.

To Mrs. Henrietta Trotter, my dear friend who showed me an ordinary person can write books. All her tips and advice helped me all along the way.

To my muse, Carl Shealy Jr., who inspired me to pursue my poetry.

Shout out to my girl Sonia Abraham who encouraged me to do a real book.

To all my kids and grandkids, Malik, Tanya, Maya, Kareem, Shemeca, Kadejra, Kara and Khrista. Also Regina, Joshua, Solomon and Elijah.

And one of my oldest friends, Antoinette Still. Someone I can always go to for spiritual help.

Also Terri Nielsen who was there for me when I needed her the most.

And all the girls on the job who suffered hearing me recite my poems.

And last but not least

My God and Savior

     Jesus Christ

Who carried me along all the days of my life and gave me the gift of a love for words.

The Poems In Order

A Deep Deep Place

It hits me in a deep, deep place.
That only my soul knows well,
Where only I really dwell,
Inside,
My heart
Where angels go.
Where life exists in itself.
Can I see how you really are?
Can I feel
How your heart gels in my hands?
Can I tell you the commands,
Of how to win me,
To woo me,
To pursue me?
To get into my heart.
It'll be a start
Of a life brand new,
For us,
Just trust.

Adrienne Crawford

A Simpler Time

A simpler time
Of long ago.
A time to discover
Oh- I don't know.
A time for me to realize
The dreams I have
Are they all lies?
Or can they ever become true?
Or vanish off plants
Like mountain dew?
Are they like flowers
That bloom and fade?
And tall grass wilting in the shade,
From a lack of water.
Do they stop growing?
Only in my heart
Is the knowing.
Of dreams impossible
To come true
Held in a hope that
Sometimes they can do
What dreams are supposed to do
Come true for me and you.

Adrienne Crawford

Be In Tuned

Tune in,
Seek solace there
Find the strength you need.
To handle all your cares
Seek the vision
Deep within your soul.
Turn inside and
Catch a ride, to reach your goal.
Hurry fast it never lasts
This peace inside your life.
Accept it now
And maybe somehow
It will show you
Where to go.
Lock into it
Accept this season
You currently occupy.
You must learn, to turn, it
Over, to a strong One you can trust.
Be all you can be,
And do all you can
To help yourself
And others,
A stand up kind of friend.

Adrienne Crawford

All Systems Are A Go

All systems are a go.
And my, I don't know
If I'll be able
To go on with this show.
Smiling
And acting like all is well.
Hell, I could win
An Oscar
Or at least an Emmy.
For my portrayal
Of me being a happy being.
Looking at you
And imparting to you
The same old lies
And alibis
About how well I am.
You are my friend and
I can't pretend
Anymore.
It's such a bore
To be smiling so falsely
Always.
Like a Miss America
Girl with Vaseline
On her teeth
To fake it.
I will make it
Work,
Somehow
For now.

Adrienne Crawford

Brand New

You're brand new to me
I'll be true to you
Open up your heart.
Don't fear
Open up your mind
I'm near
I'll be kind
Let's get clear.
I won't add to the hurt you feel.
We can kneel at the altar of our love
It's all from above.
Waiting for you.
Don't be afraid
To open up your soul
I'll make you whole.
Be free with me
And we can be
A new entity,
Entwined, enjoined together.
We'll weather, any storm
That passes by
We can try
To become one.
Let's wake up the sun
In the morn
With our love.
It'll be the norm
I can soothe away all your pain.
It won't be a strain
For me.
I love you
You see.
Let's try to be free.
It's my plea.
Baby.

Adrienne Crawford

You Need Balance

You need balance
In your life.
No time
For strife.
You need healing
In your soul.
Let love be
Your goal.
You need peace
By your side.
No more pain
To hide.
You need life
Inside your heart.
Come together
And be a part,
Of a movement to
Quiet the earth.
Let sun beams
Give you birth.
And see the hours
Passing by.
Find a mate
Give love a try.
Open your heart
And know this.
Truly, to find the right one
Can be bliss.

Adrienne Crawford

Love Abides

Love abides
Time subsides.
Words grow dim
Life is slim.
Earth keeps spinning
I keep winning.
The world moves on
I sing my song.
Life can always change
Time can rearrange.
The sun forever shines
The moon always whines.
The stars begin to show
Life has it's own flow.
And tomorrow never comes
My days are on the run.
I see you passing by
I hear you saying, why
The end has to come.
Where do we come from?
Where are we going to?
Where can we start anew?
When will the end be?
When will the birds flee?
Why is the sky blue?
Do you know what to do?

Adrienne Crawford

Movie Nights

Movie nights
Sunburn flights
A vacation in my view.
Scenic heights
Food delights
I know what I want to do.
Catch a plane
Ride a train
See the USA.
Find a show
See and know
Where you want to go.
Look to life
See it clear
Find your earthly bliss.
Seek your maker
Be so grateful
Your life consists of this.

Adrienne Crawford

And So I Go On

And so I go on
Into the night.
Asleep
I dream the dream that keeps repeating.
I stand next to you
I look into your eyes.
I feel your heat
And I repeat
I love you,
I see you,
I hear you,
In my soul
And for a minute
I am whole.
Complete as a woman
I need to feel that.
I bask in the flavor, of that
It keeps coming back.
So I surrender to the feeling
Letting it wash over me.
And I revel in the goodness of the vibes
It gives me
And know all is well.
I am a woman,
And I feel,
And my feelings are real.
And I reel at the thought of you,
But it's alright
It's only a dream, remember.

Adrienne Crawford

Busy Days

Busy days
And the snow filled haze
That descends upon my mind.
Happy chores and lovely scores,
For Christmas presents I find.
The wintry air
The coldness there.
Outside these wooden doors
Makes me want to stay in
And snuggle once again
More and more and more.
The time flies fast
The year is past.
And January 1st is near.
Let's be thankful
And oh so grateful,
And let out an awesome cheer.
God has let us
Live to see
Another time go by.
So I appreciate
I can wake,
Up with many more fish to fry.
And in the coming days
I'll see thru that haze
And begin
With fresh eyes to see.
And count my life a win.

Adrienne Crawford

Come Gently

Come gently into the world
When you awake
Let life come slowly into view.
Express gratitude
For sleep and for life.
Walk gently thru your day
Find space for quietness.
Reconnect with your God
Be gentle with others.
Your children whom you love,
And random people you meet.
Go gently to your sleep
Be grateful for the day.
Dream pleasant visions to come
Close your eyes in peace.

Adrienne Crawford

Feelings

Feelings
From deep inside
I try to hide from mine.
Impossible to do
You know it's true
I really loved you.
Where are you?
Are you here?
Are you near?
Did I make myself clear?
I cannot live without you.
I don't breathe unless you
Come into my sphere.
I'm awaiting your appearance in my life
Please show up
Just grow up
And reach up
And touch me
You will see
How greatly
I need thee To love me
Really and truly.

Adrienne Crawford

Don't Worry

Don't worry
About tomorrow
It's a new day.
Don't stress
About the weather
It's a little grey.
Don't fret about yesterday
Those deeds are done.
Do care about the future
Now let's have so fun.
Don't belittle this, now treasure
Of time right now.
Ever in the present, somehow.
Live in the moment
Be here right now
Now!
Now!
Now!

Adrienne Crawford

From Ages Past

From ages past
To ages to come.
From the deepening sky
To the morning sun.
From life on earth
To life on Mars.
From the distant cosmos
To the evening stars.
Life is expressive
See how it flows.
Life is the differences
From the yeses to the nos.
Sometimes you win
And sometimes you don't.
Life is a donut
You don't have to dunk.
Eat your confection
Dip it in your cup.
Eat a piece of chocolate
Or eat some nuts.
Eat whatever
Is set on your plate.
It may just be karma
Or maybe it's fate.
Whatever life dishes you
You still have a choice.
To chose your path
And use your voice.
Life is what you make it
Grand or not so much.
Put forth your hand
And give it your touch.

Adrienne Crawford

In Looking

In looking for someone
I found me.
In trying to find truth
I found a key.
In trying to pass time
Time flew free.
In trying to unwind
I sprang with glee.
In trying to seek peace
I let things be.
In trying to discover life
Oh, golly gee.
In seeking a path
A road I see.
In learning a way
I paid a fee.
In trying not to faint
I grew strong.
In trying to do right
I righted wrong.
I said a prayer
On bent knee.
To help others
Be all they can be.

Adrienne Crawford

Life Is A Picture

Life is a picture
A portrait painted full
Life is a measure
Never really dull
Unless you make it
Be that very way
You must conspire
To live every day
And to make a difference
To make another smile
To be the best you can
For just the little while
You inhabit earth
And live in this world
You must do your damnedest
To show your own worth
And lead the little children
On a better path
To help people
End up with a laugh,
Tell a joke or two
Smile all the time
Life is too short
To be really unkind
To one another
And not to find
Out how to help the people
In your life
To live a life
Without any strife
Life can be long
Depending on what you see
Is it a good life
Or as bad as can be?
Only you can really decide

If your life is good or bad
And if you can provide
A way to make it
Happy or sad.

Driftin' In And Out Of Sleep

Driftin' in and out of sleep
Viewing memories from the deep,
Parts of my mind
Tryin' to unwind.
Dreamin' of days long ago,
Memories held as a show.
Flashin' colors across the screen
Vivid pictures in my dream.
Streamin' like live video
Starin' at photos, that show,
Things long forgotten
And dreams that were verboten,
In real life.
Discovered why I was born
Put here on earth not to scorn.
Glad to be alive
No need to apologize.
For what I believe
And hold so dear.
I proceed only to hear, and do
Only good deeds and what I need to,
For others, realizing
Karma works.
And only hoping
To never shirk,
My duty
To myself
And others.
Helping wives and mothers
Sisters and their brothers.
Begin their life anew.
To find their self,
So true.

Adrienne Crawford

A Little Birdie Told Me

A little birdie told me
Where you live.
A little birdie told me
I can give.
You a big smile
And a big hello.
A little birdie said
That you got that flow.
A little birdie said
The sky is new.
Then he expressed
An idea or two.
A little birdie whined
I feel so blue.
Cause I'm all alone
And I need to do.
So many things
To help myself.
I need to find
A bucket of wealth.
But then birdie
Chirped right up.
There's more in
My favorite cup,
Then there is, without.
I have something
Good to chirp bout.

Adrienne Crawford

I Didn't Choose My Path

I didn't chose my path
My path chose me.
I didn't chose my life
My life found me.
I didn't chose the goal
The goal to be free.
I didn't chose the way
It opened up to me.
I didn't chose the light
Light shined on me.
I didn't seek the sun
The sun beamed, you see.
I didn't want to learn
But learning came to me.
I didn't want to rest
But in rest I am free.
I didn't want to be
Only me always me.
I didn't seek the vision
But by the vision I can see.
I didn't dream the dream
But in dreams,
Life's as it should be
I didn't search for moons
But the moonbeams follow me.
I didn't seek the journey
But my feet journeyed free.
I didn't walk these steps
But step by step I agree.
My life is an open book
For all to come and see.
But there are places reserved
Where only I can be.

Adrienne Crawford

Life Interrupts

Life interrupts.
The interruptions of life
The discussions so ripe.
The feeling so pure
The love endures.
The time is right
Senses taking flight.
Life begins anew
What to do?
Enjoy this gift
Feel the fire.
Light the way
Find your desire.
Life is good
A life so free.
Love your life
And totally see,
Your path ahead
Clear enough to travel.
Be sure which way to go
And don't unravel,
On the way
To your destiny.
Know your God prepares your way,
You see.

Adrienne Crawford

I Dreamed A Dream Of You

I dreamed a dream of you
You were a vision that came thru.
My night time sleepy dance
In my head you started to prance.
You were as smooth as can be,
Float like a butterfly,
Sting like a bee.
You made me happy in that reverie.
You were the apple falling from the tree
I picked you up and started to proceed.
To take a bite of what I need.
It was only just a dream.
That for a while was real it seemed.
And so I bid you adieu
In my sleep you were on cue.
I woke up and you were standing still
I loved you then and I always will.

Adrienne Crawford

Are We Poets?

Are we poets quite the same?
Do we sit around
And place the blame
On this blank sheet
Staring us in the face?
Daring us
To write something.
Anything.
I say stand up
Don't be bullied!
By the white, cleanliness
Of a new sheet of paper,
Staring at you
Daring you.
Be firm.
Write nothing!
Aw shucks,
That's not going to work.
My hand quickly grabs the pen
I begin to pen a poem.
So sure I will win,
And finish with a flourish.
I rush to end it all,
And send it by email
To a friend.
Hoping to cheer him up
Good luck with that.

Adrienne Crawford

In My Room

In my room
Good things transpire.
I heard the voice
Of a heavenly choir.
I heard the sounds
Of angels singing.
I saw the flight
Of doves winging.
To the moon
And back again.
You hold my heart
In your hand.
Treat it well
I'm at your command.
I've fallen fast
And cannot stand.
I'm in deep
The quick sands steep.
I'm on a limb
Not saying a peep.
I jump in the water
Diving head first.
No thought of will
I get hurt.
That's the only way
I can know.
If this love of ours will grow.
I want it, to be so.
But the future is
The only one who can know.

Adrienne Crawford

I've Been Listening

I've been listening
I've been twisting.
In the wind so free
To discover and to see.
Which way to proceed
And where I have to heed.
The next step to take
And the promises I make.
To others I must keep
And the ones to me so deep.
And live a life so good
And do exactly as I should.
Or maybe as I shouldn't
Or even what I couldn't.
Accomplish in a time
With the treasures I did find,
Installed in my mind.
Revelations from the sun
And planets on the run.
Speaking from heavenly spheres
And cloudy atmospheres.
Where angels tend to dwell
The stories they do tell.
Of life on a different plain
Invisible to the sane.
But shone to those who know
Where is the picture show.

Adrienne Crawford

I Am Loved

I am loved
And loved already.
I feel the source
I sense the steady,
Force of love
Rain down on me.
He who runs the world
You see.
Love's me more
Than you can.
Better than any man
Can love a woman.
I'm so complete.
You'd only compliment
And I repeat.
He loves me more
This I know.
And so my heart
Is filled just so.
With peace and love
And joy abounds.
His voice I hear
In heavenly sounds.
And so I need not
Worry more.
Peace is marching
Through my door.
I hear the voice
Of one who knows.
Me inside out
And so it shows.
On my face
I smile well.
Because He loves me
I can tell.

Adrienne Crawford

I Feel Tense

I feel tense.
I walk the fence with you,
I feel trouble
Is brewing.
Like a fresh pot of coffee
Between me and you.
Somehow you choose
And I lose.
Not fair
I'm not there with you,
And I don't care,
For you,
The things you do.
I choose
To leave you,
Walking to the door
As you implore me to stay.
No way, Jose.

Adrienne Crawford

Life Is A Merry Go Round

Life is a merry go round,
Round and round it goes.
Where does it stop
Nobody knows.
Life is a Ferris wheel
Way up high.
In the very heavens
So very near the sky.
Life is a roller coaster
Up and down the hills
Giving all the riders
Very many thrills.
Life is a fun house
The mirrors inside distort.
How you and I look
Making me look so short.
We look much larger
Than we really are
We look much bigger
Than a candy bar.
Life is a flying rocket
Going to the moon
We will be traveling there
Very, very soon.
Life is a water slide
We get wet as we go.
We will need to dry up
The sun will do it slow.
And this poem now ends
On this day of fun.
We must have joy in our life
And in our daily run.

Adrienne Crawford

I Hear The Breeze

I hear the breeze
Whistling thru the trees.
I want to know
Will there be a freeze?
The plants wonder
Will they be cold?
My heart expects
Someone to be bold
Enough to tell us
All about life.
And how love goes on
Into the night.
And how the green grass grows,
And how babies count their toes
And learn where is their nose.
And sometimes the sun shines
Or maybe some rain does fall.
As you recall, all the days
When snowflakes fell
From the sky
So high.
You looked up as a kid and tried
To count the stars
And put lightening bugs in jars.
And ran around summer nights
Playing with cousins in your sight,
And hopefully with whom you never fight.
And life goes on,
You sing your song
And trudge on and on.

Adrienne Crawford

Looking To Life

Looking to life
To fill you up,
Days come and go in a blaze
What's up?
Time flies
And before you know
You didn't go
Where you wanted to go.
You didn't do
What you needed to do.
You let the sands of time wind down,
You started but
You didn't finish
Or win.
The goal of your life
To find the joy.
The passion of work
You could enjoy.
And do all day
And fill your cup
Until you popped.
Happiness,
You feel thru and thru
Living your life
As you should, do.

Adrienne Crawford

I Keep Wanting To Call You Baby

I keep wanting to call you baby, But to me you don't belong.
I keep wanting to call you baby, I want to take you home.
I keep wanting to call you baby, You move me in my soul.
I keep wanting to call you baby, Your attention is my goal.
I keep wanting to call you baby, I feel you in my heart.
I keep wanting to call you baby, This is just a start.
Of a new endeavor, it has just begun.
But it feels like forever, Let's have a lot of fun.
I keep wanting to call you baby, I see you in my dreams.
I keep wanting to call you baby, And so it really seems.
That you are a true friend, we'll be pals til the end,
Of the life we lead   So please, take heed.
I keep wanting to call you baby, On me you can depend.
I keep wanting to call you baby, My heart is on the mend.
I keep wanting to call you baby, that's all I have to say.
I keep wanting to call you baby. Maybe, some day.

Adrienne Crawford

Life Is A Basket

Life is a basket
Turned upside down.
Ends in a casket
Where others frown.
Live it to the hilt
You only live once.
Drink from a jug
Every single ounce.
Know that time
Will always tell.
Just how you lived
Either heaven or hell.
You can choose
How you live.
You will be remembered
By how you give.
Give from your heart
It knows best.
When you get that feeling
In your chest.
Give from your soul
You know that's true.
It will make you happy
And not so blue.

Adrienne Crawford

Moonbeam Wishes

Moonbeam wishes
And candy kisses,
As we walk along the shore.
Ice cream dreams
And sunlight streams
By the river
Running more swiftly through.
The wandering path
Close by the edge
It winds and whistles.
Like a bird
Perched upon the hedge,
Sunny days
The dew filled haze.
In the morning bliss
Scattered showers
And raindrop spatters,
That pool in spots like this.
Starry nights
Dusk street lights
As we walk down the road,
To the home we left at dawn.
Anxious to unload
All the days happenings
We'll sup and spill the day.
After eating
We keep repeating
We're so happy
And gay.
We're thankful
For a long day
And strength to complete our tasks
We have a life
To be envied
A life that lasts and lasts.

Adrienne Crawford

Light Beckons

Light beckons
I see beyond spheres and years,
The tears
I should cry for my past life.
I hold back
No need to track past events.
When time was spent
On other pursuits.
I intuitively know
Where is my flow,
And where I want to go.
There is much to learn
To listen and dissolve.
In my brain
It feels like a strain
To try to get to know you
So I shoo you away,
Hey
It's the best I can do
For now.

Adrienne Crawford

I Luv Ya

I luv ya more than the bees love honey
I luv ya more than the bankers love money.
I luv ya more than trees like to grow
I luv ya more than water likes to flow.
I luv ya more than stars like to shine
I luv ya in this place and time.
I luv ya more than choirs like to sing
I luv ya for the joy you bring.
I luv ya more than birds like to fly
From now on, til the day I die.
I luv ya more than the dogs like to bark
You have taken ahold of my heart.
I luv ya more than bread likes to bake
This love for you I cannot shake.
I luv ya more than lions like to roar
My heart in your hands begins to soar.
I luv ya more than soldiers like to fight
I'm lovin' ya day and night.
I luv ya more than kids like to play
I luv ya in a special way
I luv ya more than the wind likes to move
You've put me in a fantastic groove.
I luv ya more than cats like to meow
I can't begin to tell you, how you make me feel
I only know
That's it's for real.

Adrienne Crawford

Life Is A Series Of Seasons

Life is a series of seasons,
Each one more precious than the last.
You move from season to season,
A line you sometimes pass.
You move from dark to light.
And from night into the day.
You cross meridians in your mind
When you begin to say,
That season last was a good one
But this one is better still,
I'll cherish every moment
On my windowsill
Where all my plants and flowers sit
Blooming as they go.
They fill the house with fragrance
As they begin to grow.
So accept the season you're in
It is the best by far.
It will help you to understand
Each day is a superstar.
In it's own right a treasure
A chance to begin again.
To start your life over
And commence to win
This new season of your life
It will be better by far,
Than any season you've lived with
Until you reach the bar.
Value all your days.
Let not one pass quickly by
The minutes come so fast
And quickly they do fly.
And turn into hours and days
Weeks and months go swifter still.
What have you accomplished?
What gives you a thrill?

Treasure the days you have
In whatever season you're in.
Only then you'll know
The reason you can win.

Adrienne Crawford

I Step Outside

I step outside at dawn
Stifling the yawn.
That tries to escape from my lips.
My hips
Walking in a easy stride.
As I measure
The steps on my path.
The race is long
The throng of fellow racers
Pacing thru the misty morning
On the road.
Trying to discover
The meaning of this life
We all want to know,
Why is the sky blue?
Why is there dew?
Why is each day new?
And what street must I
Meet, to complete
My own race?

Adrienne Crawford

Live Your Life

Live your life
On a different plain.
Seek the peace
After the rain.
Find your grace
To make peace so.
Find the path
That lets you know.
You are a creature
Moving on earth.
Being reborn
In a new birth.
Looking to the future
Although life is now.
Start the discussion
And take a bow.
Share your discourse
Handle your show.
Let others follow
The way you go.
Express yourself
In a good way.
You'll have answers
Others can say.
She really helped me
Stay my course.
Following her words
Was my choice.
Speak your mind
Positively so.
Say your piece
And say it slow.
So others can
Decipher what you mean.
Help yourself
Find your dream.
Be the queen

You really are.
Sit on your throne
Or drive your car.
Be the best ruler around
Once your feet are on
Solid ground.

Jesus

I know where I stand
In whose hands I'm held
And protected from all disease.
Please,
Understand
Where I'm coming from.
I walk among the clouds
So proud
To be a child of the King.
I cling to Him
Each day.
Knowing He is the One
That holds me up,
Thru every adversity.
I am free.
Because He
Died for me.
I'm strong
I'll live long in
His Love.

Adrienne Crawford

I've Been Thinking About You Recently

I've been thinking about you recently.
I've been wondering how you really can be?
I've been pondering about how
You're so attentive to me.
And I do appreciate
The time you spend, you see.
I'm the type of girl,
If someone does something for me,
I do recognize it
Because it shows me,
You've spent the time to think
About a woman with my pedigree.
And I realize time is valuable.
As precious as can be.
So just to let you know
I thank you.
And you are very special to me.
And I also want you to know
I think of you happily.

Adrienne Crawford

Night Falls

Night falls and shadows call
And I still recall
How much I loved you.
The sky deepens
My heart weeps and
Clouds creep in my view.
The starry night
Is just a flight
From the sunny day
The eagles flying above,
Know, the way.
And where treasures are stored
I do implore
Them to come and play.
My heart turns
My soul burns
And it is only for you,
I yearn.
My heart pounds
To the bell
That resounds
Our love will rebound
That's true.

Adrienne Crawford

I Never Thought

I never thought I'd see
A day where we ceased to be
As one, my true friend.
You're letting this come to an end.
And I will love you still,
My heart is yours until,
The end of time as we know it.
I was never able to show it
To you and for eons to come.
Only the sun will have the fun
Of knowing how I loved you,
With a love forever true.

Adrienne Crawford

I Want Someone

I want someone who thinks I'm special,
Someone who feels I'm divine.
One who knows I'm exceptional,
One to treat me so kind.
One who'll love to laugh,
At any jokes I tell.
And pretend I'm the most beautiful,
Girl in the whole wide world.
One who will send me flowers,
For no reason at all.
Just to let me know,
He'd take me to the ball.
One to send me a love poem,
Romantic words and such.
Just to tell me that,
He loves me so very much.
One just for me alone,
For my very own.
I would be so happy,
I would take him home.
To meet all the folks
Crowded round to see.
If we are compatible
As the queen and her honey bee.
One to make my eyes light up
When I see his handsome face.
One with some panache
And a masculine grace.
One who will love me forever
And a day for sure.
One to takes my cares away
To a distant port.
And to take my mind away
Like the Calgon commercial says.
One to make me remember
This life is as good as it gets.

One I can be thankful with
And share my every mood.
To love when the times are bad
And when the times are good.

Adrienne Crawford

Maybe

Maybe
Someone saw something in you
That you could do.
All you needed to
To become yourself.
Maybe just maybe
Someone saw your frame.
And could see your fame.
And that you could tame
The beasts inside.
Maybe just maybe
You don't need to fear.
You can really cheer
Your road is clear,
To go your way.
Maybe just maybe
You were sent to earth.
To show your worth
From the day of your birth,
Until now.
Maybe just maybe
You can rejoice
You have a choice.
To speak your voice
And show your talent.
Maybe just maybe
You have a gift.
That can give a lift
Whether slow or swift.
To the world.
Maybe, just maybe.

Adrienne Crawford

I Stepped Out Of Time

I stepped out of time
To another place
I stepped out of constraints
To a special grace
I stepped out of life
To an infinite space
I stepped out of earth
To a starry waste
Life is confining
Eternity is not
Life is a box
I don't like a lot
Always possibilities
On my plate
I see the future
And it looks great
This is my year
I won't hesitate
Do what I want
And not procrastinate
Do as I feel
And never be late
For the life I'll love
For it will be great
Step out of time
Into forever, wait
Leave the past behind
And be totally straight
Elevate my mind
Change my gait
Seek the higher plain
Look to the sky
And at the grain
Growing by and by.

Adrienne Crawford

No One Can Stop You

No one can stop you
From being free.
It's only your persuasion
It's the way you see.
Your perception
Is all you need
Of your life's direction.
So let it be.
Let others go
And be themselves.
Forgive yourself
It will be your wealth.
Open your mind
See a possibility.
And find the truest way
You can be happy.

Adrienne Crawford

You Feel Like Home

You feel like home
You feel like love.
You feel like a steady hand
In a glove.
You feel like a rock
Solid as can be.
I can push and
You'll be.
Like a tree
A mighty oak.
Going nowhere soon.
You feel like
A trip to the moon.
You feel like oceans
And a calming sea.
You feel like life
So precious to me.
You feel so fine
And you look so good.
Can I take you
Back to my hood?

Adrienne Crawford

Quiet The Soul

Quiet the soul
Calm the heart.
Step aside
And be apart.
Leave the sounds
Of the earth.
Learn to listen.
To the birds.
Hear them tweet
They do sing.
A sound so sweet
An offering.
Hear the sound
Grass does make.
When it grows
And takes it's place.
You cannot hear it
It's silent now.
That's the purpose
To still your brow.
And unfurrow it
Don't worry how.
Life is good
And better somehow,
When you leave it
For awhile.
Become again
A little child.
Allow yourself
The luxury of,
Being alone
To hear from above.

Adrienne Crawford

You Smiled

You smiled at me
I saw your face.
I looked at you
And beheld your grace.
You said a a word
I heard it clear.
You let me know
I shouldn't fear.
You laughed at life
And then I knew.
There'd be no strife
Between us two.
You touched me gently
On my cheek.
I'll be loving you, all week.
You made a frown
Or so it seemed.
You wanted to do more
To see me beam.
Then the smile
Came back again.
From this day forward
You'll be my friend.

Adrienne Crawford

Life Is A Mosaic

Life is a mosaic
A pattern of colored tiles.
Putting the pieces together
May take you a little while.
It's almost like a puzzle
Each part fits it's own space.
Any other piece
Would be out of place.
So see each tile as beautiful
A treasure in itself.
It will fit a perfect spot
It's presence will be felt.
Life is a long, long dream
Where your wishes can come true.
Your visions of the future
Hold pleasures if you do,
The things that you wished for
Deep inside your heart,
The plans you made can be the ones
You dreamed of
From the start.

Adrienne Crawford

I Wanted To Send You A Poem

I wanted to send you a poem
One to make you smile.
I wanted to tell you a story
Your attention to hold for a while.
I needed to tell you a tale
About a boy and a girl.
Who truly loved each other
More than all the world.
I needed to let you know
Sometimes these tales come true.
I wanted you to know about
A love just for you.
I wanted to regale with
Verses so defined.
They would remove all
Of the stress in your mind.
I wanted you to chuckle
And have a laugh or two.
I wanted you to be happy
So I would be happy too.

Adrienne Crawford

Love Is Like A Dream

Love is like a dream
Or so it seems
So real
Like the hour, when we're half asleep.
Our eyes close to peep
We're nearly asleep.
Like dusk
When the sun goes down
We nod and drop our heads
We see the moon
Coming soon
We croon
To babies
At that time
A chance to rhyme
So sublime.
It's nearly dark
And we almost part from
This world into the world of sleep, deep
We wind down to find
Strength anew, for a new day.

Adrienne Crawford

I Thought About How You Are

I thought about how you are
So sweet and kind thus far.
How attentive you seem to be
Really, really pleases me.
I always hear you laugh
It makes me happy at last.
Been looking for a while
Could you be that smile?
I've been searchin' from long before
I'll know it when thru my door,
You walk and come my way
With your special kind of sway.
Maybe, it's a go
Or maybe it's a no.
But we both realize
We both have our lives
And life is short you know
You must get into your flow.
To find your heart's desire
The feeling and the fire.
That makes you want to live
And makes you want to give.
To others who have less
And do your very best.
To give because it's right
And gives you more delight.
To be kind to a friend
Helps you more in the end.
And so I'll stop it here
Off to the working sphere.
But I'll put pen to paper
For you I'll do a favor.
And write one just for you
Because you are so new.

Adrienne Crawford

I'm Philosophizing

I'm philosophizing and testifying
To the words in my mind.
The stairs I have to climb
To reach the soul divine.
And seek the inner realm
Where treasures are at the helm.
And life goes on all day
Heart beating without delay.
And breathing brings a clue
Of what I should do.
But I'll digress for now
And then maybe somehow.
The song will be true
The one I sing for you,
And for me and others sure
I'll walk thru the right door.
And dance a fancy jig
And don a funny wig.
And eat spaghetti fast
At my next repast.
And look into your eyes
And see your surprise.
At who I have become
A rebel with a bun.

Adrienne Crawford

I Thought I Lost A Thousand Poems

I thought I lost a thousand poems
But a thousand came to me.
They rushed in, like a flood,
Into my mental sea.
My mind explored each of them
They were my children you know.
I birthed them all in the time
When they wanted to show
Others, a good direction
And how to get into flow.
Where your life just proceeds
And you get that special glow.
When you know where you're going
And where you're headed still,
And you know you can choose
A path with your best will.
I thought I lost a thousand rhymes
But a thousand came to me.
They flew right into my mind
Like a bird into a tree.
They belonged to me alone
Because I was their mom.
They decided to show up
In the nick of time.
In the eons to come forth
They all will work out fine.
All the thoughts and memories
Will have had their prime.

Adrienne Crawford

On The Day

On the day you were born
The sun came out to say.
This boy child will grow up
In a very special way.
He'll be strong and mighty
A king, among men.
A wise and generous person
A good and loyal friend.
He'll be smart as a whip
And love from deep within.
He'll show others how to live
And how to be a man.
He will father children
Who will love him well
And love his pretty wife
And treat her very swell.
He's made his mother proud
Of the man he has become.
He was a very happy child
Born under a wintry sun.

Adrienne Crawford

Spinning

Spinning in space
No trace of a place.
I journey to a distant shore
I tour
The sandy beach
Til I reach, the dunes
Just out of site
I fight back the tears
That fall in tiers
Down my face.
Unfazed by your disdain
As the rain
Continues from my eyes.
Why you say do I cry?
This living alone
Is no bone for a dog
But a choice thrust upon me
As I sort thru
The corners of my life.
Filled with the fumes
Of a former love.
The one who filled my life, gone.
No song in my heart
As I depart
This here and now.
Somehow I'll win.
How
I can't see.
But I'm sure
In future
I'll be free.

Adrienne Crawford

When I Think

When I think about my life
About how it all began.
I think about the day
I began to win.
When I chose for myself
To speak my piece.
I chose my own wealth
To live my life with ease.
I moved into my space
I filled all the rooms.
I stepped onto my place
Underneath a shining moon.
I looked to the heavens
And let out a huge sigh.
I breathed in the life
From God on high.
I ceased from strife
It came from above.
And lived my life
Filled with love.

Adrienne Crawford

If You Could Be Mine

If you could be mine
That would be quite nice.
I could serve you lemonade on ice.
I could be the cook
You could start the grill.
I could be the maid.
You totally fill the bill.
As the man of the house
You could be the cheese.
I could be the mouse
I could do as I please.
I could take a nibble
Just a little taste
You're better than kibble
When I taste your face.
We could play jax
Or maybe pickup stix.
If I had a lollipop
I'd give you a lick.
We could play doctor
I would be your nurse.
You could do embalming
I would drive the hearse.
We would get along together.
We'd play so well.
No matter what the weather
All would be swell.

Adrienne Crawford

I Wear Pajamas

I wear pajamas all day
And drink coffee by the jug.
I eat sweets and don't pay
Attention to what's happenin' above.
The news passes me by
And the weather I don't try,
To listen and find out
Cause today I'm not out and about.
Did it flood round your way?
Did ice storms come to stay?
Did earthquakes shake you up?
And volcanoes start to erupt?
Did hurricanes send you running?
And tornadoes have you gunning?
And trying to escape their path,
Did you frown instead of laugh?
Those things I don't know about
Cause I didn't wander out,
Or turn the TV on
Don't know about any storm.
For me that is the norm.
So please don't clue me in,
That would be a sin.
I'm snug as a bug in a rug
From the news causing this din.

Adrienne Crawford

Life Is A Song And A Prayer

Life is a song and a prayer
On your knees, you'll go there.
Life is a song you sing
With the joy, you bring.
Life is an offering
To the God of your choice.
Give your best all day long
And use your greatest voice.
Life is a prayer you pray
You speak to the heavens above.
Life is the work you do
Out of a heart of love.
Life is a choice you make
Of what to do each day.
Life is the value of your time
When you do what it is you say.
Do it with vim and vigor.
Do it with all your might.
Don't be afraid of tomorrow
It is only a tiny slice
Of the ages of eternity.
Each will blend into another.
While on earth you must do
All you can to uncover,
The things really important
To you, and you and you.
Do what you decide
Is most important for you.
Live your life to the fullest
The best is yet to come.
Help one another
To have some major fun.
See if you can try
To give it your best shot.
Know you'll always be
Much more than you are not.

Adrienne Crawford

I Was Put Here

I was put here
To live, to love, to laugh
And not be discouraged
At the paths others take.
No mistakes on my part
Everything done
Whether serious or in fun
Was just to let me know
I can glow, and grow and show
The world my talents.
I'm bent on a path
To walk the walk and now just talk the talk.
Times flies
And I have no alibis
About where I've been.
I was born to win,
And be all I need to be
To help you too know God loves you.
And so I go on
I sing my song
All day long and into the night also.
And I know the world is good
As it should, be.

Adrienne Crawford

Lovely Lines

Lonely lines on a pristine paper
Words written lost in a vapor
Two phrases spoken I need to savor
For sure.
The light shined for a little while
The picture painted was my style
The photos taken so beguil-
Ing -yes.
As to be in an art gallery
Where paintings are reviewed happily
And you sup on canapes with celery
So good.
And the moon dances still,
Stars bend to their will
And the cold wind produces a chill
For real.
And children play outside
They go on with their kiddie rides
Running soon as the street lights
Come on.
And life goes on in the Jects
Where real life rejects
Those with no dough and no respect
So wrong.

Adrienne Crawford

Surface People

Surface people
They stare you in the face.
But you only get a trace
Of who they really are.
You sense their words
The ones you heard
Only tell a part of their heart.
They look at you
Like you're a cow colored blue.
Like they look thru you.
And you see them on the surface.
Like the face of the moon
Cratered up and far away.

Adrienne Crawford

The Shadows Fall

The shadows fall
I don't recall
A time when all
I wanted to do,
Was love you fine
And be your bride,
Stand at your side
And see how you do.
I was your girl,
In the other world
I was your pearl
And I shone.
I honed my skills,
You fit the bill
You were my thrill
So I chilled.
I illed also when
You took your stand
And demanded I love you.
You can't understand
And demand I love you.
You can't demand
Love in your hand.
So, be a man
And understand
I can't be with you
So sorry.
The quarry's gone.
The end of this song.

Adrienne Crawford

If Your Yes Is Yes

If your yes is yes
And you're at your best.
You'll be fine
And right on time,
With whatever you plan to do.
See your life
Thru rose colored glasses,
As it passes thru the prism.
Multicolored rainbows
That show you the way to go.
You'll never know
Until you try,
Before you die.
Follow your dream
Or so it will seem
A waste of your life.
Find the time
To give it your best shot.
So your life will not
Be lost
Such a heavy cost.

Adrienne Crawford

I'm Seeing

I'm seeing
Where my heart goes.
Where love flows
I only know
What I can do for me.
I can't see
What you need to do for you.
You're a mystery
And somehow I'll be
Able to solve
Your case.
In any case
The race is to the swift.
I can't lift
Your heavy heart.
You're,
Apart from me
And that's good.
I need space
To trace
The face of you,
On paper,
So later
I can see you as you
Really are,
A star
With immense capacity
For reality.
You can be who
You truly are,
A superstar.

Adrienne Crawford

Meditation

Meditation
The key to really knowing me,
I see the future
In blocks
Of tales turning,
The scales
On a life brand new.
I turn inward
To find the keys
Of life to connect
To the source.
Of course,
To quiet my mind
And to find peace
And rest.
The best is yet to come.
I run from the pace
Of modern life.
So rife with rituals
And phones, texts.
What's next?
Who's trending?
I'm pretending I really care.
I don't, and I won't.

Adrienne Crawford

I'm Feeling You In A Special Place

I'm feeling you in a special place
Only time will tell a trace
Of what transpires here.
You're the best in this sphere.
On this earthly plain
Where beasts are killed and slain.
My heart's an open book
Come nearer and take a look.
See inside, my pulse is strong
I'll love you short or love you long.
I'll love you day and into night
Your heart with mine will take flight.
And traverse planets and the moon
We'll sing to each other a special tune.
We'll sail the seas
And oceans well.
On a ship that has a bell.
To toll the hours
That we pass together
No matter the storm
Or any weather.
I'll pray for you
And you for me.
Call me up and we can see
If this love can truly be.
Or will you find
I'm not really me
The one you want or
The one you see.

Adrienne Crawford

Life

Life
Short or long
Is to be lived.
And to be embraced
And chased.
Squeeze every good thing out
Every minute
You can win it.
And proceed on your goal.
To fill your soul's desires
Be on fire.
Be alive
Thrive.
And enjoy yourself
It will be your wealth
And increase.
And fill your needs
Please
Proceed.

Adrienne Crawford

I'm In A Melancholy Mood

I'm in a melancholy mood
I chose to brood
On this hour of pain.
The rain
Falls on this plain.
Sustained
By the winds of change.
I rearrange the furniture
In my mind.
Time to find
A place to unwind
And disconnect
From the life
I formerly lived.
What I would give
To see you live
And thriving
And being strong.
It's been so long
I can picture
You now
Somehow walking your way.
And hey
I say hello.
Do you know which way to go?
I don't think so.

Adrienne Crawford

Men Don't Change

Men don't change
They're all the same.
They always want
To know your name.
They start out good
And then get lame.
They all want to play
Their silly games.
They want to access
Things inside.
Things I really need to hide
They all want to know
The Baby Girl.
But you must
Travel thru the layers.
To get to the inner court
I'm a fortress
And a fort.
You must knock
The walls down.
I put up
To help you drown.
In the moat
Before the door.
Of my heart
I do implore.
You to swim
The water's fine.
Except for gators
In the brine.
They'll eat you up
If you can't swim.
To get to me
You must have vim,
And vigor.
Eat a nutritious diet.
To get to me

You'll need to try it.
Try to find the key
To unlock
The heavy door
To my heart you see.

Adrienne Crawford

I Was Listening To The Music

I was listening to the music
All inside my head.
I was listening to the music
Laying on my bed.
I was listening to the music
It felt so very good
I was listening to the music
I didn't know I could.
Hear all the instruments
Playing one by one.
Hearing all the sounds of them
They played and were some
Of the best sounds I've heard
In quite a while.
All the very best
Such an engaging style.
Of the notes they played
Musicians are so free.
To play their versions of things
Only they can see.
Of rhymes and chords and melodies
Dancing in their brains
We hear it when they play
All their lively strains.
Each of us hear it
In a different way.
The music goes thru all, our sense pathways.
Before it reaches to our hearts
We hear with different ears.
Each of us digest the sounds that only we can hear
And all that is OK
For each and every one,
Is so very different
Just relax and have some fun
No need to fuss and cuss
Because you like this song and I like another.
I am your sister and you are my brother.

So listen and be happy
We all can choose
Which song we like the best
We don't have to lose.

Adrienne Crawford

Monkey Shines

Monkey shines
Childish rhymes,
The days of our youth.
Playing outside
Til it got dark.
Catching lightening bugs
Tag you're it.
Hide and seek
Looking thru my fingers
Just a peek.
Seeing you under
The mulberry bush.
Hopscotch and jump rope
Candy canes and jelly beans.
Easter eggs and
Childish screams.
When I scraped my knee,
Mom came running
She kissed it all better you see.
And I was off and running.
Again.
Way back when.

Adrienne Crawford

Mystery And The Discovery

Mystery, and the discovery
Of how love can be.
I can only see you
As you are,
Driving a car
Reaching far
For a distant rendezvous.
Will I see you?
Will I be blue?
Never really knowing you
Will the truest you come forth to shine?
And take your time
To unwind
The cassette tape of your heart?
So I can see all your flaws
And guffaws
And the jaws of life encapsulating you
With the terms and germs of ideas
From distant shores.
I implore you
Come forth
Shine on me
And let me see
The glory and story of you.

Adrienne Crawford

What Has Gotten Into You

What has gotten into you?
What has gotten into me?
That makes you want to laugh
And me to say he he.
Life sometimes is funny
Sometimes, not so much.
But a good laugh will help you
Feel the Master's touch.
He's in your life everyday
You may not feel Him near.
But He's right beside you
Making sure you don't fear.
Look to Him for comfort
Or for guidance still.
He promised never to leave you
And I know He never will.
He holds your hand in bad times
And in good times He walks beside.
Sometimes He carries you
When the pain you can't abide.
He is the one who leaves
The footprints in the sand.
He is your God and Savior
Jesus Christ, The Man.

Adrienne Crawford

Printed in the United States
By Bookmasters